Christmas Jokes

Johnny B. Laughing

DEDICATION

This book is dedicated to everyone that loves a funny joke.
Laughter is one of the best gifts you can give. It always puts a smile
on your face, warms your heart, and makes you feel great.

CONTENTS

FUNNY CHRISTMAS JOKES

Q: What did they call Santa after he lost his pants?

A: Saint Knickerless!

Q: What's Scrooge's favorite Christmas game?

A: Mean-opoly!

Q: Did you hear that one of Santa's reindeer now works for Proctor and Gamble?

A: It's true. Comet cleans sinks!

Q: Who delivers cat Christmas presents?

A: Santa Paws!

Q: What game do reindeer play in their stalls?

A: Stable-tennis!

Q: What can Santa give away and still keep?

A: A cold!

Q: What do you give a train driver for Christmas?

A: Platform shoes!

Q: Who sings "Love me tender," and makes Christmas toys?

A: Santa's little Elvis!

Q: What was the hairdresser's favorite Christmas song?

A: Oh comb all ye faithful!

Q: Why is Christmas just like a day at the office?

A: You do all the work and the fat guy with the suit gets all the credit!

Q: Who brings the Christmas presents to police stations?

A: Santa Clues!

Q: Who is never hungry at Christmas?

A: The turkey because he's always stuffed!

Q: Why does Santa like to work in the garden?

A: Because he likes to hoe, hoe, hoe!

Q: If Santa Claus and Mrs. Claus had a child, what would he be called?

A: A subordinate claus!

Q: What did Mrs. Claus say to Santa as they were looking out their front window?

A: Looks like rain dear!

Q: Who delivers elephants Christmas presents?

A: Elephanta Claus!

Q: What reindeer can jump higher than a house?

A: They all can! Houses can't jump!

Q: What's fat and jolly and runs on eight wheels?

A: Santa on roller skates!

Q: Which of Santa's reindeers needs to mind his manners the most?

A: Rudolph!

Q: What did Santa shout to his toys on Christmas Eve?

A: Okay everyone, sack time!

Q: What is the difference between the Christmas alphabet and the ordinary alphabet?

A: The Christmas alphabet has no el!

Q: What is the cow's holiday greeting?

A: Mooooory Christmas!

Q: What does Santa say when he is sick?

A: OH OH NO!

Q: How do cats greet each other at Christmas?

A: A furry merry Christmas and happy mew year!

Q: What's the best thing to put in a Christmas cake?

A: Your teeth!

Q: What do vampires put on their turkey at Christmas?

A: Grave-y!

Q: What's the most popular wine at Christmas?

A: I don't like sprouts!

Q: Why did the reindeer wear sunglasses at the beach?

A: Because he didn't want to be recognized!

Q: What nationality is Santa Claus?

A: North Polish!

Q: What's Santa called when he takes a rest while delivering presents?

A: Santa pause!

Q: What do you get hanging from Santa's roof?

A: Tired arms!

Q: Who delivers presents to baby sharks at Christmas?

A: Santa Jaws!

Q: What songs do Santa's gnomes sing to him when he comes home freezing on Christmas night?

A: Freeze a jolly good fellow!

Q: What do you have in December that you don't have in any other month?

A: The letter D!

Q: How do you make a slow reindeer fast?

A: Don't feed it!

Q: What do you call a man who claps at Christmas?

A: Santapplause!

Q: How did the chickens dance at the Christmas party?

A: Chick to chick!

Q: What's a ghost's favorite Christmas entertainment?

A: A phantomime!

Q: What do you get if you deep fry Santa Claus?

A: Crisp Cringle!

Q: How many chimneys does Santa go down?

A: Stacks!

Q: What does Santa suffer from if he gets stuck in a chimney?

A: Santa Claustrophobia!

Q: Why did your boyfriend return his Christmas tie?

A: He said it was too tight!

Q: What does Dracula write on his Christmas cards?

A: Best vicious of the season!

Q: What does Santa call that reindeer with no eyes?

A: No-eyed-deer!

Q: What did Dracula say at the Christmas party?

A: Fancy a bite?

Q: How do sheep in Mexico say Merry Christmas?

A: Fleece Navidad!

Q: What happens to you at Christmas?

A: Yule be happy!

Q: Why couldn't the butterfly go to the Christmas ball?

A: It was a moth ball!

Q: What do gnomes fear most about Christmas?

A: They're afraid Santa will give them the sack!

Q: Why couldn't the skeleton go to the Christmas Party?

A: He had no body to go with!

Q: What do you call a letter sent up the chimney on Christmas Eve?

A: Black mail!

Q: Did you hear about Dracula's Christmas party?

A: It was a scream!

Q: Why is a cat on a beach like Christmas?

A: Because they both have sandy claws!

Q: What did Adam say on the day before Christmas?

A: It is Christmas, Eve!

Q: Why was Santa's little helper depressed?

A: Because he had low elf esteem!

Q: Why does Santa go down chimneys?

A: Because they soot him!

Q: How does Santa Claus take pictures?

A: With his North Pole-aroid!

Q: Why is it so cold at Christmas?

A: Because it's in Decembrrr!

Q: What's Tarzans favorite Christmas song?

A: Jungle bells!

MAZE #1

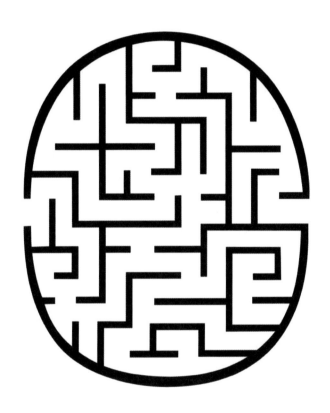

MAZE #2

MAZE #3

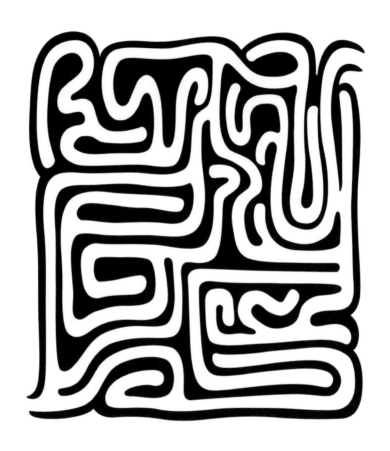

MAZE #4

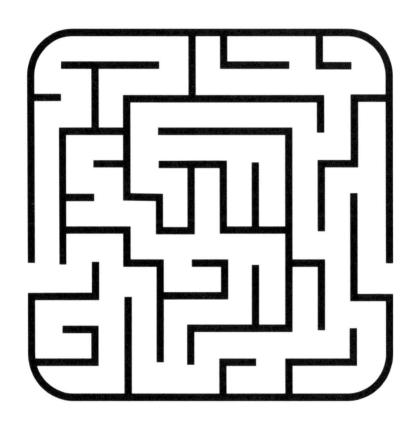

MAZE #5

MAZE #6

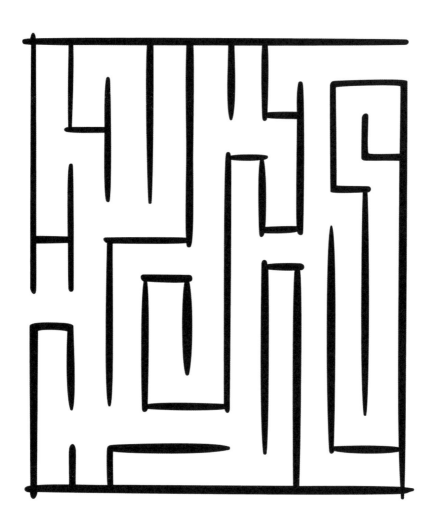

MAZE #7

MAZE #8

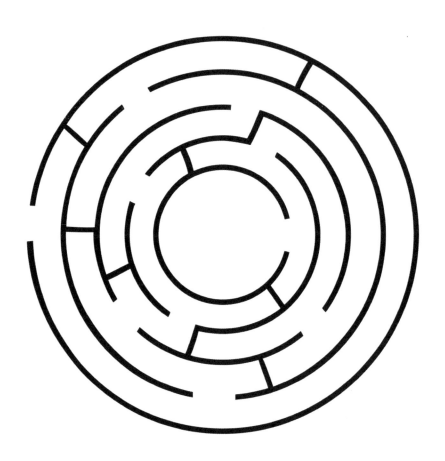

MAZE SOLUTIONS 1-4

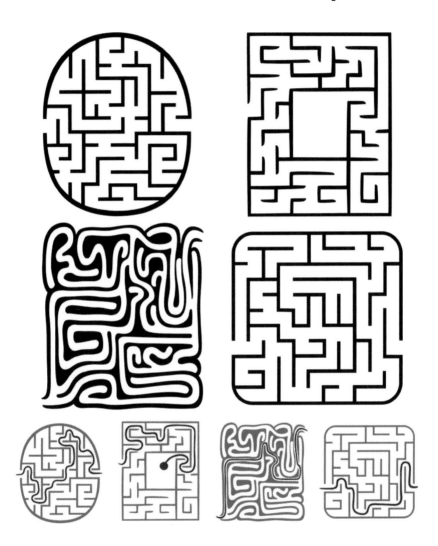

MAZE SOLUTIONS 5-8

ABOUT THE AUTHOR

The Joke King, Johnny B. Laughing is a best-selling children's joke book author. He is a jokester at heart and enjoys a good laugh, pulling pranks on his friends, and telling funny and hilarious jokes!

For more funny joke books just search for
JOHNNY B. LAUGHING on Amazon

-or-

Visit the website:
www.funny-jokes-online.weebly.com

Printed in Great Britain
by Amazon